Adoption God's Way

Written by
Kristen Pita

Illustrations by Issy Pita and Skylar Pita

ISBN 979-8-88540-369-6 (paperback)
ISBN 979-8-88751-658-5 (hardcover)
ISBN 979-8-88540-370-2 (digital)

Christian Faith Publishing
832 Park Avenue
Meadville, PA 16335
www.christianfaithpublishing.com

Printed in the United States of America

I dedicate this book to my husband, our three children, and our past foster children whom I will love forever. This book was inspired by the Holy Spirit because it's too good to have come from me. My hope is to encourage whoever reads these pages to reflect, repent, and reset. Thank You, to my Lord and Savior, Jesus Christ, for saving a wretch like me to write a book like this.

~Kristen Pita

1

Hello, friends, do you know that God our Creator is willing to become God our Father? He wants to become our Heavenly Father because He loves each one of us very much. This love that He offers to us is called adoption, and it's one of the ways that His perfect love is made visible on earth as He reigns in heaven. There are two kinds of adoption under God. One is earthly adoption, and the other is heavenly adoption.

But as many as received Him, to them He gave the right to become children of God, to those who believe in His name. (John 1:12)

Every person was created by God and given a soul. We cannot see our soul just as we cannot see God while on earth, but both exist. Our soul was made by God to live forever either with God in His kingdom of heaven or separated from God in a place called hell. God is love, and through the overflow of His love for His human creations of male and female, He gave each person a soul. This soul has the capacity to love just as God loves, unconditionally and unending.

And the Lord God formed man of the dust of the ground, and breathed into his nostrils the breath of life; and man became a living being. (Genesis 2:7)

So God created man in His own image, in the image of God He created him; male and female He create them. (Genesis 1:27)

God also blesses each person with the gift of free will, which means we can freely choose to love God as our Heavenly Father through faith in His Son, Jesus Christ, or we can freely choose not to. God wants us to love Him back, but He doesn't force us to. He gives us life and then lets us choose what we will love more in our heart, Him or His creations. This choice directly affects our eternity.

> But without faith it is impossible to please Him, for he who comes to God must believe that He exists and that He rewards those who seek Him. (Hebrews 11:6)

Living on earth means we are born separated from God in heaven. The kingdom of heaven is a perfect place. Earth is not a perfect place. All human beings mess up sometimes, which is called sin. God hates sin. God has an unending love, but He didn't create us to sin. We use our free will and choose to sin. God doesn't want us to continue being separated from Him, so He made a way for all people to be reconnected back to Him. This is called being born again or being saved. God has one perfect, sinless Son named Jesus Who came to earth to pay the penalty for our sins. The penalty for our sins is death. We were not created to die but to live with God forever on earth, but sin destroyed that perfect plan. This world teaches that good people will go to heaven to be with God after we die, but this is not true because no person is good. We all sin, and sin can't go to heaven. So God gave us Jesus, the only sinless One.

For all have sinned and fall short of the glory of God. (Romans 3:23)

Jesus loves us as God loves us. Jesus brought us the good news of salvation that is found only in Him. This is called the gospel. To explain the good news of Jesus, we must first understand the bad news about us. As children born on earth, we all have earthly parents. Everyone has sinned, including our parents. Every person has a mom and a dad, but because sin affects all of us, it makes life here on earth very hard. Some parents find themselves unable to raise the children whom God created through them. But all children who are created are a gift and designed with a special purpose. Every person was created to know God, to love Him, and to make Him known on the earth. Most people don't know that God loves them. Sin keeps people from believing in Him. Sin is disobedience to God and His Word. Sin is the opposite of God's love. Sin caused the whole world to become broken starting with the sin of Adam.

> Jesus answered, "I am the way and the truth and the life. No one comes to the Father except through Me." (John 14:6)

Adam was the first human being whom God created. Adam let God's enemy, Satan, who is also called Lucifer or the devil, deceive him and his wife Eve in the garden of Eden, which was here on earth thousands of years ago when God made the earth. Adam and Eve let Satan into their minds by listening to his lies about God. Adam and Eve started to believe that they could be like God. This is called pride, and it's the sin that got Satan kicked out of heaven and sent him here to rule earth. Satan, whose name is also Lucifer, used to be God's most devoted archangel who led beautiful music in heaven for God. Lucifer became jealous of God's power and wanted to run things himself. Lucifer didn't love God. He loved himself and his own way of thinking, which is called pride. Pride is a sin that Satan uses today on all people so they will choose to believe that they know better than God on how to rule their own life. But God being so rich in His mercy loves to restore things that have been broken by sin.

The great dragon was hurled down—that ancient serpent called the devil, or Satan, who leads the whole world astray. He was hurled to the earth, and his angels with him. (Revelation 12:9)

When earthly families become broken, God provides something very special called adoption. Adoption is when God can take the emotion of love and make it visible on earth. Everyone can see real love when God is a part of it, just as everyone can see the destruction of sin when God isn't the desire of a person's heart. Sin brings forth death, the Bible says—spiritually, physically, emotionally, and eternally. But love is the supernatural glue that fixes the broken hearts and lives in this world.

> Above all, love each other deeply, because love covers over a multitude of sins. (1 Peter 4:8)
> But God demonstrates His own love toward us, in that while we were still sinners, Christ died for us. (Romans 5:8)

15

Earthly adoption is when adults who want to be a mom or dad decide to show their love for children by choosing to bring them into their family. This is a personal invitation to join their family on their journey through life together as if that child had been born from those adults. These very special grown-ups are called adoptive parents. They adopt and choose this child personally because they already love them. Something similar is also offered by God to all people. It's called being adopted into the family of God or becoming God's child. Adoption is at the heart of God's story for the world. God gave us His story through the Holy Bible.

God decided in advance to adopt us into His own family by bringing us to Himself through Jesus Christ. This is what He wanted to do, and it gave Him great pleasure. (Ephesians 1:5)

Religion that God our Father accepts as pure and faultless is this: to look after orphans and widows in their distress and to keep oneself from being polluted by the world. (James 1:27)

Holy Spirit

Why are earthly adoption and spiritual adoption so unique? Because both reveal the love of God for all people. God wants to be with us forever as our Heavenly Father, but sin destroyed His perfect plan for mankind on earth. But our good Creator God made one perfect way to restore our heart, save our soul, and rescue us from continuing on earth as children of wrath. We all are born on earth as children of wrath because God does not become our Heavenly Father unless we receive His free gift of salvation. We don't have to push God away as the world tells us to. He isn't here to harm us but to help us. God sends His Holy Spirit to live inside of anyone who wants to love and obey Him. The Holy Spirit is our Helper through life. Putting your faith into God's Son, Jesus Christ, adopts you into God's heavenly family and washes away your sins. If the penalty of our sins is not paid for through salvation in Jesus, then we each will face judgment by God when we die.

> Then Peter said to them, "Repent, and let every one of you be baptized in the name of Jesus Christ for the remission of sins; and you shall receive the gift of the Holy Spirit." (Acts 2:38)

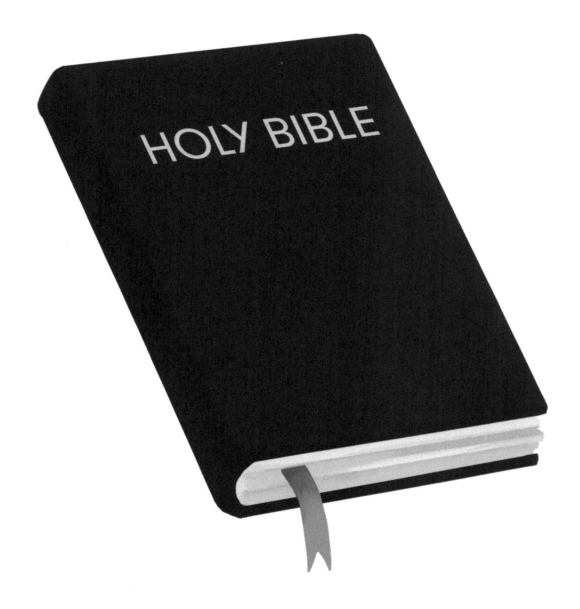

Have you been adopted by an earthly family? Have you been adopted into God's heavenly family? Adoption is a huge part of God's story of the world. God left us His story inside the Holy Bible. It tells us how the world began, how man and woman fell into sin, and how God sent a Savior to earth to save anyone who wants a restored relationship with Him. God's restoration plan for the earth is all about the beautiful choice of adoption that He offers to us all, in His spirit and in our flesh. God's Word says that Jesus will be coming back to earth one day to collect His believers so they can be a family forever being children of God.

> When everything is ready, I will come and get you, so that you will always be with Me where I am. (John 14:3)
>
> For the Lord Himself will descend from heaven with a cry of command, with the voice of an archangel, and with the sound of the trumpet of God. And the dead in Christ will rise first. (1 Thessalonians 4:16)

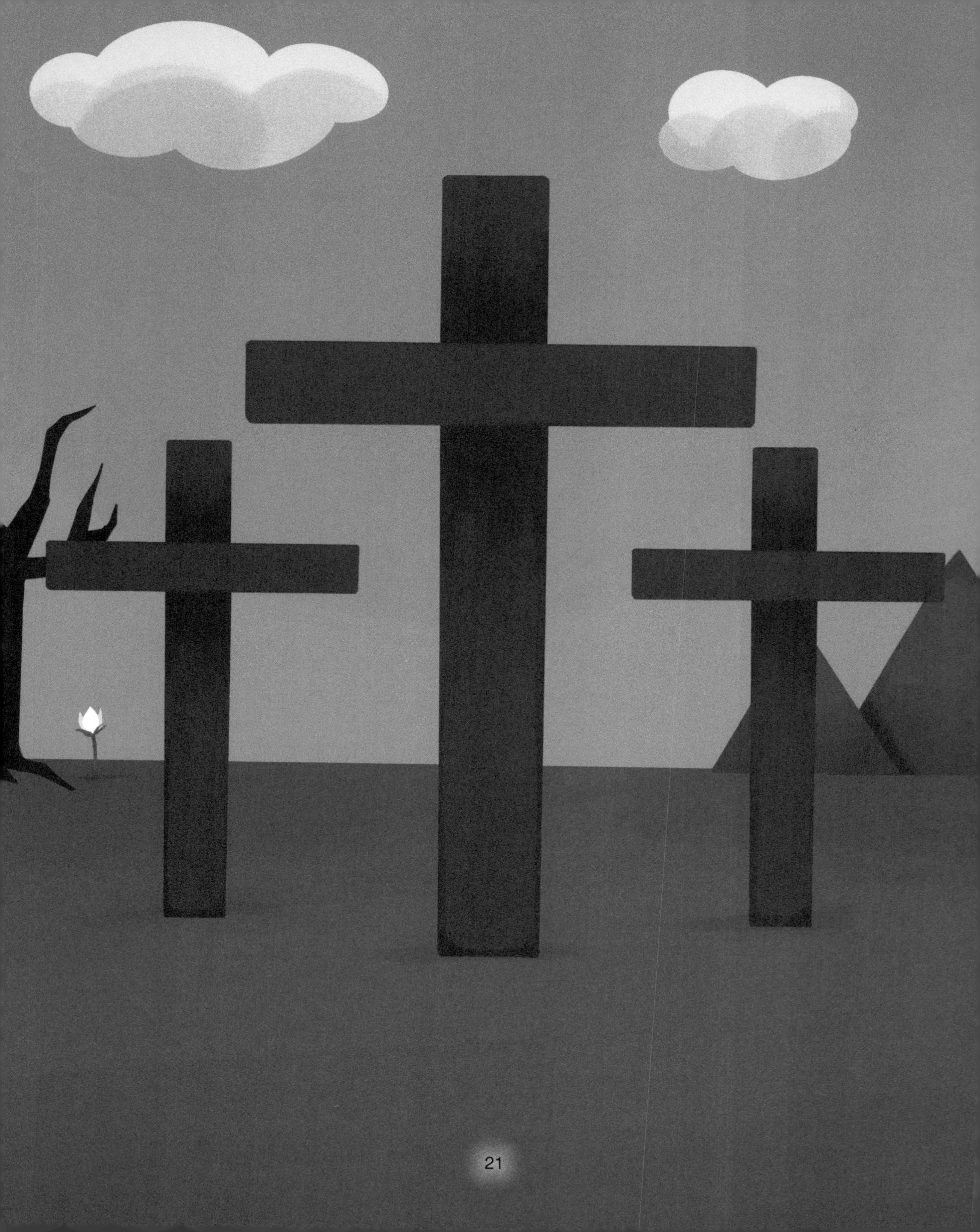

Jesus brought the good news of the gospel to earth as He demonstrated a sinless life for thirty-three years before His crucifixion. He gave up His human life on a cross to pay the penalty for our sins. Jesus made the only way for ours sins and our parents' sins to be forgiven. "The wages of sin is death," God's Word says, but Jesus took the death that we deserve so His blood could cover over the sins *of those who put their faith in Him for their salvation*. Jesus rose to life three days later as He said He would, defeating death and the grave, proving that He was God in the flesh.

> That if you confess with your mouth, "Jesus is Lord," and believe in your heart that God raised Him from the dead, you will be saved. For it is with your heart that you believe and are justified, and it is with your mouth that you confess and are saved. (Romans 10:9–10)

Father

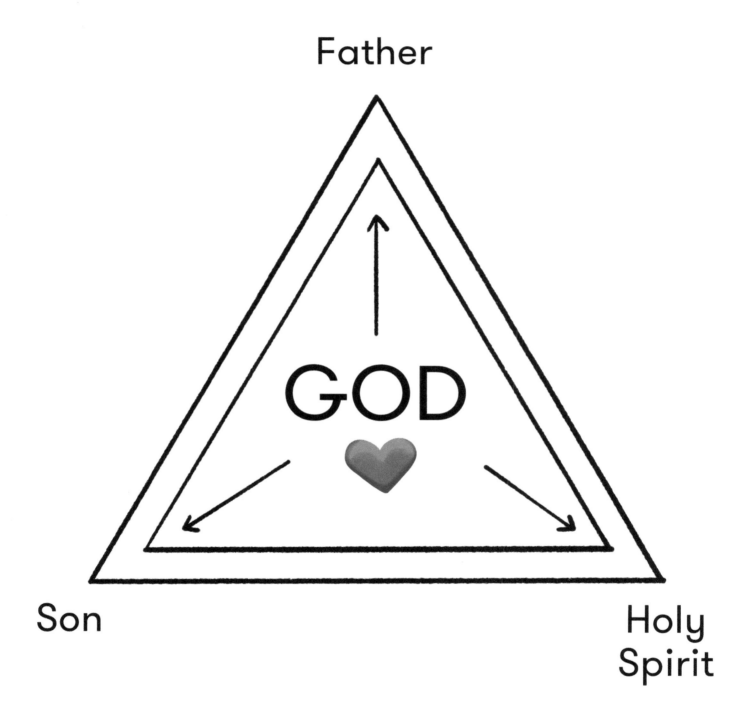

GOD

Son

Holy
Spirit

God is three persons in one. He is God the Father, God the Son, and God the Holy Spirit. This perfect Trinity holds all things together in the world. Gravity, your heartbeat, life, and death are all under the authority of God. The Trinity or Godhead sits outside of our universe, outside of time and space. God is all-knowing and all-powerful. God is eternal. He is the beginning and the end. He is love and justice. Jesus returned to His throne in heaven after His crucifixion and resurrection where He reigns today, but one day He will return to earth to raise up His believers to the Father in heaven for eternity.

Go therefore and make disciples of all the nations, baptizing them in the name of the Father and the Son and the Holy Spirit. (Matthew 28:19)

Most people don't realize it, but everyone is up for adoption. Our soul is from God in heaven, but it lives here temporarily on earth. It won't stay here long, but it will go somewhere forever. Where do you think souls go when the body dies? It's a good question to think about at a young age because most adults try not to think about it, which is part of that pride sin mentioned before. God's truth is the only truth that matters since He is the One Who holds creation together every day. The world, which is under the control of Satan, tries to make people follow their feelings. But God's Word says that we should never trust our feelings. Feelings are always changing by our environment, which is deceptive. God's truth is never changing. His Word is the rock on which we are all called to build our lives. Our soul was made to worship God. It's up to us to decide.

> Therefore everyone who hears these words of Mine and acts on them, may be compared to a wise man who built his house on the rock. "And the rain fell, and the floods came, and the winds blew and slammed against that house; and yet it did not fall, for it had been founded on the rock." Everyone who hears these words of Mine and does not act on them, will be like a foolish man who built his house on the sand. "The rain fell, and the floods came, and the winds blew and slammed against that house; and it fell—and great was its fall." (Matthew 7:24–27)

God says that our soul will either reunite with Him in heaven or stay disconnected from Him as it was on earth. A lost soul, unsaved by Jesus, will spend eternity with their spiritual father, Satan. Satan will spend eternity in a terrible, loveless place called hell. The worst part is that God won't be there. Eternity apart from the goodness of God is not what God wants, but it's what many people choose with their gift of free will. Those who choose to know about God in their mind but not receive Him in their heart will not be children of God. Loving God doesn't mean you get health, money, and all your dreams to come true. That would be selfish. Loving God means you get to have a personal, unbreakable relationship with Him, which is better than anything this world has to offer. Followers of the Savior, Jesus Christ, don't have an easy life. God's Word declares that. They are hated by the world because the world first hated Jesus. *Friends with the world* means enmity with God, the Bible says.

> Yes, and all who desire to live godly in Christ Jesus will suffer persecution. (2 Timothy 3:12)
>
> Enter through the narrow gate. For wide is the gate and broad is the road that leads to destruction, and many enter through it. But small is the gate and narrow the road that leads to life, and only a few find it. (Matthew 7:13–14)

Just as earthly parents want us to love them as they love us, God is the same way because we are made in His image. Our love is proven through our obedience and actions to our earthly parents and to our Creator God Who wants to be our Heavenly Father. The fruit of our faith in Jesus will be seen in our new "born-again" lives turning away from sin. We are unable to turn away from sin without God's strength and power living inside of us. This power is called the Holy Spirit. A Holy Spirit-filled person will love what God loves and hate what God hates. Any sin that controls the heart leads your life astray. Sin will lead you away from God and the purpose that He has for your life. Those who humble themselves before the Lord Jesus Christ, acknowledging that they are a sinner unable to save themselves, will find freedom out of the prison of serving the world, no longer under the control of the evil one known as Satan, the devil.

Whoever has been born of God does not sin, for His seed remains in him; and he cannot sin, because he has been born of God. (1 John 3:9)

31

Satan wants to adopt you and take you away from God. He hates God and tries very hard to trick people into not trusting our Lord. Satan is prideful and wants to win more souls to hell. It's a competition to him. He knows that God loves you, so he doesn't want you to love God back. A relationship with God through Jesus is the most powerful thing a person can have. God being with you and in you doesn't make you a god, but it does grant you access to God's strength to break any evil, sinful option that Satan gives you in life. Satan will tempt you in many sinful ways to make you resist God's Word. Jesus spoke more about His warnings of hell than He did about heaven. Jesus is so serious about you repenting and loving God that He died for you. He offers salvation, a new heart that beats for Him that possesses the same Holy Spirit of God that rose Jesus from death to life. A saved soul goes from dead in sin to alive in Christ. When you are free from the shackles of sin, you can fight sin every day and *win*!

> And you He made alive, who were dead in trespasses and sins, in which you once walked according to the course of this world, according to the prince of the power of the air, the spirit who now works in the sons of disobedience, among whom also we all once conducted ourselves in the lusts of our flesh, fulfilling the desires of the flesh and of the mind, and were by nature children of wrath, just as the others. But God, who is rich in mercy, because of His great love with which He loved us, even when we were dead in trespasses, made us alive together with Christ by grace you have been saved, and raised us up together, and made us sit together in the heavenly places in Christ Jesus, that in the ages to come He might show the exceeding riches of His grace in His kindness toward us in Christ Jesus. For by grace you have been saved through faith, and that not of yourselves; it is the gift of God, not of works, lest anyone should boast. For we are His workmanship, created in Christ Jesus for good works, which God prepared beforehand that we should walk in them. (Ephesians 2:1–10)

ETERNITY

Adopted
by God

Adopted
by Satan

In this life you can be adopted by God, or you can remain adopted away from God. Either way God will love you, but only one way gives you the ability to love Him and others as He does. If you are earthly adopted, congratulations! You are chosen. If you chose Jesus, congratulations! You are saved and adopted into the family of God. Now walk in the newness of a redeemed life, in the likeness of Jesus Christ. Adoption is an invitation into a different life, *not a perfect earthly life* but a life under the love and guidance of our perfect God. Life on this side of heaven is never going to be perfect because perfection lives in heaven and we live on earth, which is under the control of Satan and destroyed by sin. Your purpose is to seek God and receive Jesus. The meaning of life is resting in the contentment of that truth. We are all up for adoption. Some people are just blessed by getting two of them, spiritually and earthly. Both adoptions make God's love visible on earth. Who adopted you?

> Therefore lay aside all filthiness and overflow of wickedness, and receive with meekness the implanted Word, which is able to save your souls. But be doers of the Word, and not hearers only, deceiving yourselves. For if anyone is a hearer of the Word and not a doer, he is like a man observing his natural face in a mirror; for he observes himself, goes away, and immediately forgets what kind of man he was. But he who looks into the perfect law of liberty and continues *in it,* and is not a forgetful hearer but a doer of the Word, this one will be blessed in what he does. (James 1:21–25)
>
> For God so loved the world that He gave His only begotten Son, that whoever believes in Him should not perish but have everlasting life. For God did not send His Son into the world to condemn the world, but that the world through Him might be saved. "He who believes in Him is not condemned; but he who does not believe is condemned already, because he has not believed in the name of the only begotten Son of God. And this is the condemnation, that the light has come into the world, and men love darkness rather than light, because their deeds were evil. For everyone practicing evil hates the light and does not come to the light, lest his deeds should be exposed. But he who does the truth comes to the light, that his deeds may be clearly seen, that they have been done in God." (John 3:16–21)

About the Author

Kristen Pita is a born-again Christian who has lived her whole life in Florida. She has been a wife to Bernard for the past twenty-one years and a mother of three children. After hearing the real, sin-confronting gospel of Jesus Christ and receiving Him as her personal Lord and Savior at thirty years old, Kristen and her husband, Bernard, changed everything about how they lived their lives, made decisions, and raised their kids. Kristen started homeschooling her children using Christian curriculums, and their family began to take in foster children again after a ten-year hiatus from it. They loved and cared for fifteen foster kids (in total) over the course of five years. During the past twelve years on this side of conversion and salvation, Kristen has experienced being adopted into God's family and has eternal life awaiting for her in His heavenly kingdom made possible through Jesus. She also adopted one of her foster children whom God loves very much and He allowed to be a part of her earthly family. Through both of these two very different kinds of adoptions, Kristen has seen God's love for all mankind and the restoration plan that He offers to anyone who wants to receive it. Finding Jesus and diving deep into a Christ-centered life inspired Kristen to write this book. She is just a simple mom with only a high school education and thirty years of unknowingly living her way and not God's way, who stopped running from God and started running to Him every day. If a book like this had been read to her as a child, it could have saved her from a lot of confusion, rebellion, and pain. But God works all things for the good for those who love Him and are called according to His purpose. This is a different kind of children's book, unlike any other, and Kristen knows it's not from her but from the Holy Spirit to reach any child or any adult willing to hear God's truth—unfiltered, not watered down. Anyone reading this book should feel confronted because that's what the real gospel does; it confronts, convicts, and converts sinners from lost since birth to saved and sanctified. You shall hear the truth, and the truth shall set you free.

.

Milton Keynes UK
Ingram Content Group UK Ltd.
UKHW051349060324
439038UK00005B/12